This poem was written

on behalf of the American people

on the occasion of the death of

Nelson Mandela on December 5, 2013,

at the request of the U.S. Department of State.

BY MAYA ANGELOU

AUTOBIOGRAPHIES
I Know Why the Caged Bird Sings
Gather Together in My Name
Singin' and Swingin' and Gettin' Merry Like Christmas
The Heart of a Woman
All God's Children Need Traveling Shoes
A Song Flung Up to Heaven
Mom & Me & Mom

ESSAYS
Wouldn't Take Nothing for My Journey Now
Even the Stars Look Lonesome
Letter to My Daughter

POETRY
Just Give Me a Cool Drink of Water 'fore I Diiie
Oh Pray My Wings Are Gonna Fit Me Well
And Still I Rise
Shaker, Why Don't You Sing?
I Shall Not Be Moved
On the Pulse of Morning
Phenomenal Woman
The Complete Collected Poems of Maya Angelou
A Brave and Startling Truth
Amazing Peace
Mother
Celebrations
His Day Is Done

CHILDREN'S BOOKS
Poetry for Young People
My Painted House, My Friendly Chicken, and Me
Kofi and His Magic

PICTURE BOOKS
Love's Exquisite Freedom
Now Sheba Sings the Song
Life Doesn't Frighten Me

COOKBOOKS
Great Food, All Day Long
Hallelujah! The Welcome Table

HIS DAY IS DONE

HIS DAY
IS
DONE

A Nelson Mandela Tribute

MAYA
ANGELOU

RANDOM HOUSE

NEW YORK

Published in the United States by Random House, an imprint and division of Random House LLC, a Penguin Random House Company, New York.

RANDOM HOUSE and the HOUSE colophon are registered trademarks of Random House LLC.

Photograph credits are located on page 45.

LIBRARY OF CONGRESS CATALOGING-IN-PUBLICATION DATA
Angelou, Maya.
His day is done : a Nelson Mandela tribute / Maya Angelou.
pages   cm
ISBN 978-0-8129-9701-9
eBook ISBN 978-0-8129-9702-6
1. Mandela, Nelson, 1918–2013—Poetry. I. Title.
PS3551.N464H57 2014   811'.54—dc23 2013049202

Printed in the United States of America on acid-free paper

www.atrandom.com

246897531

FIRST EDITION

To all the world's citizens,

who lost a friend

when President Nelson Mandela died

Education is the most powerful weapon you can use to change the world.

—NELSON MANDELA

HIS DAY IS DONE

His day is done,

Is done.

The news came on the wings of a wind

Reluctant to carry its burden.

Nelson Mandela's day is done.

The news, expected and still unwelcome,

Reached us in the United States and suddenly

Our world became somber.

Our skies were leadened.

His day is done.

We see you, South African people,

Standing speechless at the slamming

Of that final door

Through which no traveler returns.

Our spirits reach out to you:

Bantu, Zulu, Xhosa, Boer.

We think of you

And your Son of Africa,

Your Father,

Your One More Wonder of the World.

We send our souls to you

As you reflect upon

Your David armed with

A mere stone facing down

The Mighty Goliath.

Your man of strength, Gideon,

Emerging triumphant

Although born into the brutal embrace of

Apartheid,

Scarred by the savage atmosphere of racism,

Unjustly imprisoned

In the bloody maws of South African dungeons.

Would the man survive?

Could the man survive?

His answer strengthened men and women

Around the world.

In the Alamo in San Antonio, Texas,

On the Golden Gate Bridge in San Francisco,

In Chicago's Loop,

In New Orleans' Mardi Gras,

In New York City's Times Square,

We watched as the hope of Africa sprang

Through the prison's doors.

His stupendous heart intact,

His gargantuan will

Hale and hearty.

He had not been crippled by brutes

Nor was his passion for the rights

Of human beings

Diminished by twenty-seven years of

imprisonment.

"**Education is the most powerful weapon you can use to change the world.**"

Nelson Mandela
LLB. UNISA, 1989 . LLD. (h.c.) UNISA, 1999.

Even here in America

We felt the cool

Refreshing breeze of freedom

When Nelson Mandela took

The seat of the presidency

In his country

Where formerly he was not even allowed to

vote.

We were enlarged by tears of pride

As we saw Nelson Mandela's

Former prison guards

Invited, courteously, by him to watch

From the front rows

His inauguration.

We saw him accept

The world's award in Norway

With the grace and gratitude

Of Solon in Ancient Grecian courts

And the confidence of African Chiefs

From ancient royal stools.

No sun outlasts its sunset

But will rise again

And bring the dawn.

Yes, Mandela's day is done,

Yet we, his inheritors,

Will open the gates wider

For reconciliation.

And we will respond

Generously to the cries

Of the Blacks and Whites,

Asians, Hispanics,

The poor who live piteously

On the floor of our planet.

He has offered us understanding.

We will not withhold forgiveness

Even from those who do not ask.

Nelson Mandela's day is done.

We confess it in tearful voices
Yet we lift our own to say:

Thank You.

Thank You, Our Gideon.

Thank You, Our David.

Our great courageous man.

We will not forget you.

We will not dishonor you.

We will remember and be glad

That you lived among us

That you taught us

And

That you loved us

All!

PHOTOGRAPH CREDITS

frontispiece AP Photo / Theana Calitz-Bilt

2 Media24 / Gallo Images / Getty Images

6 Apic / Getty Images

8 Keystone / Getty Images

11 Media24 / Gallo Images / Getty Images

12 Jürgen Schadeberg / Getty Images

16–17 AP Photo / Greg English

20–21 Helifilms / Getty Images

22 AP Photo / David Brauchli

26 Gérard Julien / Getty Images

28 Joe Alexander / Getty Images

30–31 AP Photo / Denis Farrell

34 AP Photo / David Brauchli

37 Dave Hogan / Getty Images

38 Mike Hewitt-FIFA / Getty Images

41 Media24 / Gallo Images / Getty Images

43 Trevor Samson / Getty Images

ABOUT THE AUTHOR

Poet, writer, performer, teacher, and director
MAYA ANGELOU was raised in Stamps, Arkansas, and
then went to San Francisco. In addition to her bestselling
autobiographies, beginning with *I Know Why the Caged Bird
Sings,* she has also written five poetry collections,
including *I Shall Not Be Moved* and *Shaker, Why Don't You Sing?,*
and two cookbooks, *Hallelujah! The Welcome Table* and *Great
Food, All Day Long,* as well as the celebrated poem "On the
Pulse of Morning," which she read at the inauguration
of President William Jefferson Clinton, and "A Brave
and Startling Truth," written at the request of the
United Nations and read at its fiftieth anniversary.
She lives in Winston-Salem, North Carolina.